Lyricist/Poet
Jimmy D Robinson

Welcome to

Rock the World

Jimmy D. Robinson

Contents

Come on let's

Up above the stars
Sails the light

You are not in a
Better place
Than when
Your dreams
Come alive

Painted is a
Love song
That takes
Your breath away

Come to me
Let me
Be your savior

Your voice
The moon

Keep
forever
THE LIGHT
My dreams

Take me away
Be with me

PLEASE DON'T DIE

So many roads
I've traveled
Some of the time
I was wrong
I couldn't stop
The crime
It stole my time
Lost so many days

Please don't die
Mom
Don't leave me
Your voice
Your love
In my heart
Forever
You helped me
Through
The storms

How can I
Ever
Thank you
Enough

Please don't go

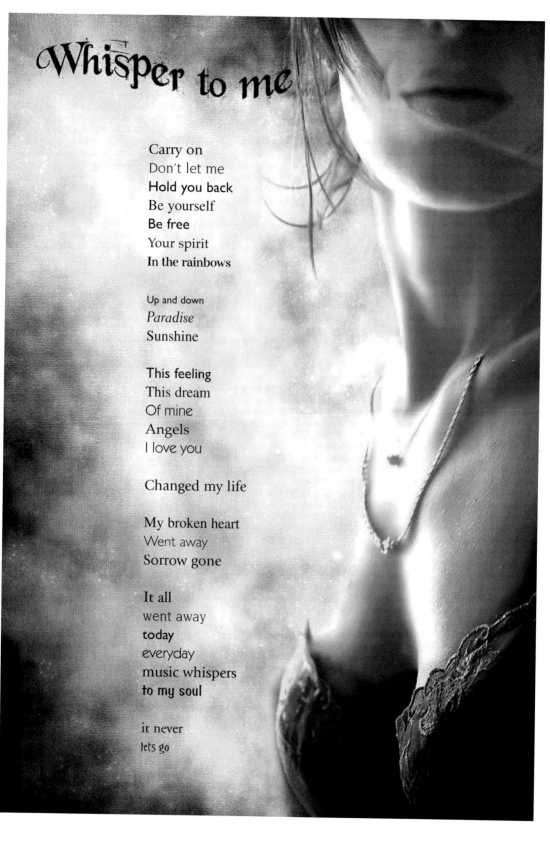

Whisper to me

Carry on
Don't let me
Hold you back
Be yourself
Be free
Your spirit
In the rainbows

Up and down
Paradise
Sunshine

This feeling
This dream
Of mine
Angels
I love you

Changed my life

My broken heart
Went away
Sorrow gone

It all
went away
today
everyday
music whispers
to my soul

it never
lets go

To feel
The stars
You must
Be yourself
No matter how
Just be
True

Many many many
Years
I was
Tortured
I was not free

I let go
Made every
New day
Bright
Love
Is free
Give it
To every human
Don't be afraid
Walk
The red carpet

With every day
Music stands
Stars they shine
But people
Make this land

The Red Carpet

THERE I AM

There I am
Everyday
There is a
Whisper
That follows
The sun
For every star
Life begins
Underneath the sky
Music begins
To take away
The loneliness

On top of
Every mountain
A soldier cries
For freedom

Today will
Today is

Every dream
I hold
Shall stand
Higher
Than an angel
Whose smiles
Brighten this sand

There I am

Again
Again
Again

The dream is real
Jimmy
Yesterday is gone
The music is alive
To make
Everyday beautiful

Hope love destiny
Shelter
Your spirit

The dove
Can fly

The breeze is low

Sunlight
Wakes the morning

God
Always a whisper
In my soul

Music
Is on the earth
It grabs
The mind
And lets it
Break free

To be
All
To be

Your soul is free

HOPE LOVE DESTINY

My, my

Little apple
On the tree
Little angel
In the sky

Little bit
Of music
Makes my
Dreams
Come alive

Little cricket
In the grass
Little moon
In the sky
The joy
Of life
Is in my eyes

Little sand castle
On the beach
Little fish
In the sea

Thank you
God
For all the
Beautiful
Things
On this earth

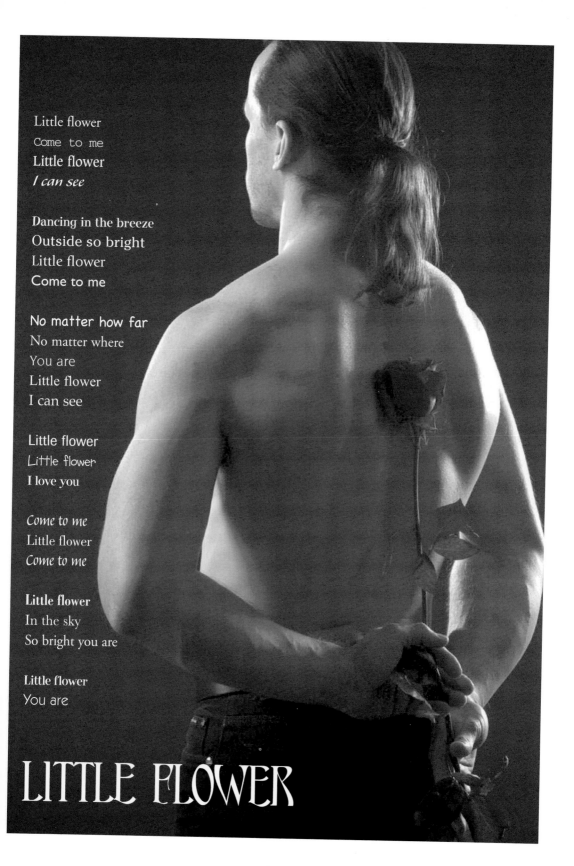

Little flower
Come to me
Little flower
I can see

Dancing in the breeze
Outside so bright
Little flower
Come to me

No matter how far
No matter where
You are
Little flower
I can see

Little flower
Little flower
I love you

Come to me
Little flower
Come to me

Little flower
In the sky
So bright you are

Little flower
You are

LITTLE FLOWER

YOU THINK THAT

Just because
I couldn't
Doesn't mean
I can't
Make tomorrow

It took
Many years
I was lost
It took
A thousand years
Nothing was
I was never
Alone
Some day
My life
I'm okay

You think that
I couldn't
But I can
I did

My dreams
Are alive
Music is alive
I did it
Freedom at last
Thank you
GOD

Truly is

The sunshine
Has guided me
To a world
I only
Dreamt of

Peace
To create
The music
Of life

Never look back
Hold yourself up
Make it happen
Say goodbye
To all that
Brought darkness
Your way

Use your dreams
To make life
All it can be

Love yourself
Show the world

Till the end
Of time

Imagination is me

All the games
The lights
The show
Many times
I fight
I dream
I sleep
I wake up

Together we can
Any fool knows
We can
Your voice
Is my savior

Movie stars
The future
Many lies
We are alive

Imagination is me
Til
I die
Cannot stop it
Never will
Ancient star
Lose yourself
Let it go
Give it a chance
Explode

Find the one

In the eye
Of freedom
The people stand
And walk free

Close your eyes
And dream
Enter heaven
Love the earth

On the wings
Of stars
**Your fate is in
The distance**
Experience life

On that
Willow tree
An owl sings
And brings
Harmony to
The sun

Life begins
Life is good
Everlasting is peace

Turn around
And watch
The angels
They are the
Mirror in your soul
Giving your heart
Freedom

Begin life
Little dancer
Begin life

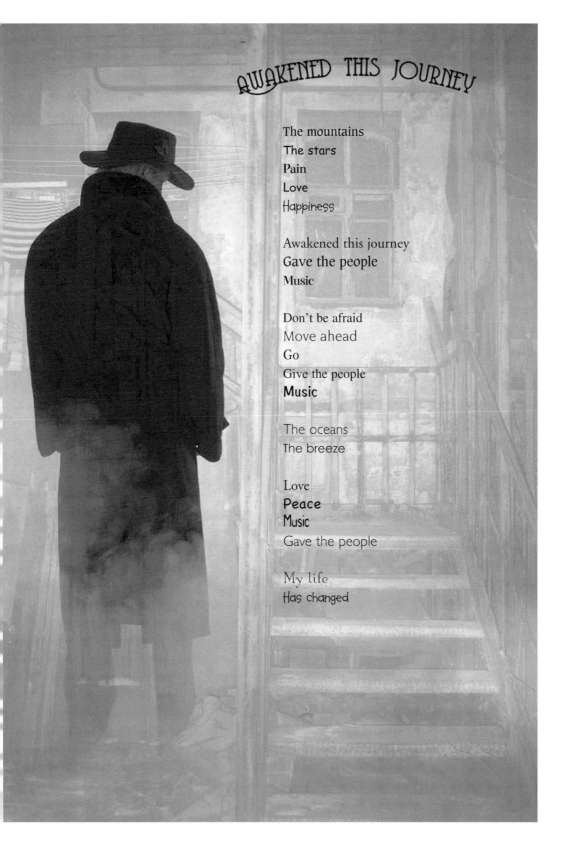

AWAKENED THIS JOURNEY

The mountains
The stars
Pain
Love
Happiness

Awakened this journey
Gave the people
Music

Don't be afraid
Move ahead
Go
Give the people
Music

The oceans
The breeze

Love
Peace
Music
Gave the people

My life
Has changed

Escape from

Seven
Nine
Thirty-three
Hold on
2010

I can
Do it
Make your life better

The storm
Apple trees
Black cats roam free
Make the forest
Grow the
Gifts of life

Angels
2050
Sky above
A whisper from
God

I'm music
3001
The world
Is free

Open your eyes
Get on my wings
Let's fly way
Little dove
Come with me

Life is
Finally free

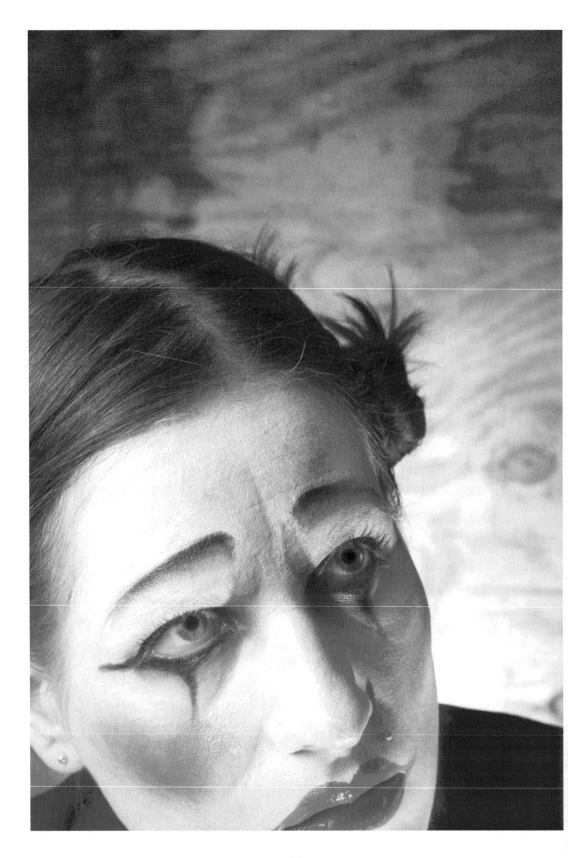

frozen tears

Frozen tears
Wake up my
Soul in the morning
Shadows disappear

Life is music
As we
Gather
And start the show

So I ask you
I want you
To know me
There to be
Let's be free

All we share
No hurt
No pain
You bring me
Wishes
Dreams come true
I need you
Frozen tears

Told my life

Too much
To drink
Sorrow touched
The purple flowers
In the rain forest

Like yesterday's dreams
Sound
Told my life
Awaken

Gift of joy
Brought love
To the journey
This soul of mine

Too much
Of anything
Is trouble

Ask the angels
Ask the rain
Ask the sky

CAVARELLI

PARIS NEW YORK CHICAGO

FORMA
DOS HOMENS

On and on
My life
Has become
A dream
Come true

GOT THE DEVIL
Out of
My hands

The joy
I now share
Sprinkles my soul
With music

On and on
Tomorrow
I go

Time is
On my side
Relax my feet
Paint the sky
With diamonds

Higher than
Any mountain
Peace drapes
My soul
Fantasies
On and on

Free
That's me
Jimmy

On and on

Sweet candy

Attention
Desire
You
You are me
Silence
Whisper
Can't hold back
I must be
Heard

To make this
Heaven
Must have meaning

Don't go
You and me
Can't turn back
Sweet candy
Angels in the sky

Life is here
Must not
Waste time

Sweet candy

Life

Just white doves

Broken all the rules
Changed my life

No hurricanes
No fires
Just white doves
Flying my music
To the sky

The mystery of life
Is the beauty
Of my soul

No demons no darkness
Just paradise

The poetry
Has changed
My life
It has danced my soul into
The hands of god

He makes
The fairytales
Sway
In these
Blue eyes

At midnight

I'd like to
Take you
Where the sky is blue
To where
My love
Never ends

Like the rainbows
Up high
How long can
We be together

Till the
End of time

You are my dream
Come true

Come with me
Till heaven
Touched my soul
Made me wake up

Spanish eyes
I can never
Let you go

You are
You are
My dream
The blue sky
I always hold

Show me down

Could it be
That I
Love you

Close your eyes
Come to me

Like the
Sky so blue
Bless the earth
Bless the people
Touch my hand
Come to me

Live free
In the land
United States
To Moscow
Iran to Africa

Freedom
Come
Let it be
Never
Slow me down
Hold my hand

Give Me

Give me
Give in
Read between
The lines
Break the stone
Silence awakens
The birds

Many lives
Alive to say
Give me words
Upon the castle
Be strong
Read the words
Of god
Give him
Your love

Every breath
You take
Makes the
Music
Awaken
The forest

Give me
Give in
Never let go

Like the leaves

Like the leaves
That fall
From a tree
My love
My desire

Like the moon
That burns bright
So happy
I am

Can't go back
Never can

That Latino
Song
Makes my
Soul
Come alive
And melt
The earth
In my soul

Four
Five
Six
Time never stops

Your heart
My soul
Forever

I Got This Feeling

I got this feeling
We're gonna
Make it

Even though
The waves part
I can't help but
To see
You and me
On the moon
Let's sail away
Or even
On a long journey
You and me
Let's be friends

I got this feeling
It's going to
Be okay
You and me
Forever
Even through
The dark clouds
You sail me away
Come on
Let's go
You and me

Blue ocean

Nine
Ten
One
Eight
Life
I do appreciate

Awake in the morning
Bright sunshine
Takes my body
Takes my soul
Lets it
Dance free

To be
To be
All to be
Give it your all
Make everyday
Free

Nine
Ten
One
Eight

Life is beautiful

Never let go
Make the song embed freedom

Make the children
Hold the hand
Of god

Make music jimmy
Touch the soul...touch the spirit

The rain the sun
Winter forest green

Ocean waves dance
To the beat of harmony

Mend my feet
Never let go

Dance naked in the sky of love

Harmony touches the hand of time
Wash away fear

Rose petals...yellow tulips

Make music jimmy

The world will dance...people will sing

Your soul is the freedom
That mends the earth

Never let go

Rock the world

The End

Love,
Jimmy

Library of Congress Cataloging in Publication Data

Robinson, D. Jimmy

Rock the World—1st ed.
Jimmyland Corporation

ISBN: 978-0-9792672-1-5
0-9792672-1-8 Trade Paper AC (USA), AC (GBR) Jimmyland Corporation

Printed in the United States of America

About the author

IMMY D. ROBINSON's highly praised works have earned him a sterling reputation in the world of publishing and music. His books have been awarded to the presenters and nominees of the Grammy Awards, the Radio Music Awards, the American Music Awards, the World Music Awards, Night of 100 Stars, and the Latin Grammy Awards. Widely recognized as one of today's most prolific writers, Robinson's poems, musical stories, lyrics, and songs reflect the tragedies he has endured, and the triumphs overcoming them. Penning his words with stark reality, writing of the human condition—loneliness, love, desperation, and hope—Robinson uses his craft to convey his belief that there is always room for change and improvement. His celebration of life comes from years of hardship which taught him valuable lessons. It is by sharing these experiences that Robinson hopes to enlighten his readers and send the message that it's never too late, that hope does spring eternal, and that life is truly what you make it.